HEIFETZ *Collection*

POLONAISE BRILLANTE No. 2
FOR VIOLIN AND PIANO

HENRYK WIENIAWSKI Op. 21

Critical Urtext Edition

Edited by Endre Granat

LAUREN KEISER
MUSIC PUBLISHING

POLONAISE BRILLANTE No. 2
for Violin and Piano

HENRYK WIENIAWSKI, Op. 21

4

5

8

10

12

Fine.

Otakar Ševčík Series

In 1881, Otakar Ševčík, the 29 year-old newly appointed professor of the Kiev Conservatory, forever changed the way violin technique would be studied with the publication of his Op. 1, Violin Left-Hand Technique. Nearly fifty years after the appearance of this ground-breaking work, Ševčík's pioneering spirit took him in the new direction of writing repertoire-specific exercises. His method of teaching included the writing of short exercises that addressed a specific technical skill. Ševčík analyzed a concerto, or a virtuoso showpiece, and isolated the inherent technical problems in order to focus on one issue at a time. Gradually, the student would put the puzzle pieces together and be able to successfully perform a difficult work in its entirety.

Each edition includes a solo violin part, a piano accompaniment and the Analytical Studies written for the particular piece. These Analytical Studies and Exercises have been out of print for over seventy-five years. This new printing of these repertoire-specific Ševčík exercises is now available for an entirely new generation of violinists. Accompanying each volume is a modern edition of each selected work by our editors, Endre Granat and Stephen Shipps.

OTAKAR ŠEVČÍK OP. 16
Wieniawski Scherzo-Tarantelle with Analytical Studies S511012

This edition is based upon years of study with Editor Stephen Shipps' teacher, Josef Gingold. Gingold studied the Scherzo-Tarantelle with Eugène Ysaÿe who in turn studied it directly with the composer, Henryk Wieniawski. Practical suggestions from Wieniawski are marked *ossia* in the violin part. The original manuscript and first edition published by Freidrich Kistner of Leipzig were consulted in making this the first ever edition to combine a modern version of the violin part with the historic and timeless exercises by Ševčík.

OTAKAR ŠEVČÍK OP. 17
Wieniawski Violin Concerto in d minor with Analytical Studies S511014

The Violin Concerto in d minor op.22 shows Wieniawski the composer in full maturity. The thematic material ranges from the beautifully lyrical first movement to the fiery *a la Zingara*. The virtuoso violin part is brilliantly written. The composer first presented this concerto in 1862 in St.Petersburg. Though the performance was a rousing success, Wieniawski rewrote and condensed the piece during the next six years. In 1868 he performed the work in its present form. This edition is based on the original orchestra score and violin piano reduction printed in 1870 by Schott in Mainz, Germany.

OTAKAR ŠEVČÍK OP. 18 & 25
Brahms Violin Concerto in D Major with Analytical Studies S511017

Johannes Brahms dedicated his only Violin Concerto to the great Hungarian violinist, Joseph Joachim. Joachim's suggestions have been sought by the composer for creating the solo part. At the same time he wrote a Cadenza that met with Brahms' approval and is perhaps the most often performed cadenza of the Concerto. This edition is the first to unite the critical Urtext versions of the Concerto, the Cadenza by Joachim, and the corresponding Ševčík op. 18 and op. 25 studies.

OTAKAR ŠEVČÍK OP. 19
Tchaikovsky Violin Concerto op. 35 in D Major with Analytical Studies S511013

In 1893, Leopold Auer finally returned to Tchaikovsky's Violin Concerto that he had refused to premiere despite the work being dedicated to him. Nonetheless, Auer published an edition of the work with substantial revisions and cuts that catapulted it into the mainstream of the violin concerto repertoire. The unique aspect of this edition is the Violin part which includes both the original and the Leopold Auer edition. This publication presents the first opportunity for performers to utilize both versions to create their own unique interpretation of this great work.

OTAKAR ŠEVČÍK OP. 20
Paganini Violin Concerto No. 1 in D major with Analytical Studies S511016

After being out of print for over 75 years, Ševčík's practice guide to Paganini's ultimate display piece for violin and orchestra is available for the first time with this modern and corrected publication. This Urtext edition includes a new violin part prepared from the manuscript with practical applications and suggestions throughout, as well as a corrected cadenza of Emile Sauret, edited by distinguished violin artist and professor Stephen Shipps.

OTAKAR ŠEVČÍK OP. 21
Mendelssohn Violin Concerto in e minor with Analytical Studies S511011

This critical Urtext edition of Mendelssohn's Violin Concerto is derived from both the original manuscript score and the first published version by Breitkopf and Härtel. The editor has resolved the minor differences between these two sources. This edition reunites the concerto with the accompanying exercises by world renowned pedagogue, Otakar Ševčík, for the first time since its initial publication. These repertoire-specific exercises address each measure of this entire concerto and suggest solutions for its technical difficulties.